This edition published in 1996 by
Tiger Books International PLC, Twickenham

Photographs:
PPWW Plant Pictures World Wide, Daan Smit
Text:
Nicky den Hartogh
Translation:
Tony Langham
Concept, design and editing:
Boris van Dobbenburgh
Typesetting:
Mark Dolk/Peter Verwey Grafische Produkties
Color separation:
Unifoto PTY LTD, Cape Town
Production:
Agora United Graphic Services bv, 's-Graveland
Printing and binding:
Egedsa, Sabadell, Spain

ISBN 1-85501-825-X

INTRODUCTION

Photographs do not reveal any of the ebullient social life which was a feature of the pleasure gardens of seventeenth- and eighteenth-century palaces. Paintings and engravings illustrate what is missing nowadays in the carefully restored historical gardens: the comings and goings of coaches and horsemen in the palace courtyard, an audience waiting around an ornamental pool where a spectacle is being performed, ladies and gentlemen engaged in courtly conversation, the ladies wearing crinolines, the gentlemen elegantly wigged and hatted. They stop in admiration by a fountain, a rare plant, a beautifully adorned garden pot, and gather in groups to discuss the beauty of a statue recently positioned at the intersection of two straight paths. The liveliness of the scene seems to depend more on the people than the plants. The gardens themselves form a static ensemble, an architectural space dominated by straight lines and governed by the strict laws of geometry and symmetry. They were designed in accordance with the same structural principles as the adjacent palace or castle, and, like the buildings they served for the reception of important visitors. Political issues were discussed in the gardens, the affairs of state were decided there, and plots were hatched, compromises made, and spectacular celebrations were organized. The whole entourage was primarily intended to confirm the owner's status. The gardens had to impress friends and enemies alike, and were a visiting card for the powerful.

During the seventeenth and early eighteenth centuries – the Baroque era – garden architecture throughout Europe was influenced by the French style. It had developed to become an art form in its own right, and often more money was spent on it than on furnishing a house. In many cases the gardens were designed with the co-operation of architects, water engineers, decorators, sculptors and gardeners.

The buildings and gardens had to form an unbroken unity. Aerial photographs and, in particular, old engravings with a bird's eye perspective, clearly show the way in which the gardens and the main building are linked by a dominating central axis which runs from the front courtyard, seemingly through the middle of the palace, and then bisects the gardens along their entire length. With this main axis as a guideline, straight paths and walkways form a system of axes within which all the areas of the garden and the ornaments are combined to form a whole. The largest ornamental pools with the most beautiful fountains and striking statuary are located at the places where the main and transverse axes cross. Drawings sometimes illustrate how these axes continue into the surrounding landscape as avenues, far beyond the actual gardens, and how the surrounding countryside forms part of the design as a whole through the use of viewpoints and perspectives.

Flat, rectangular flowerbeds – known as "parterres" in imitation of the French example – lie on either side of the main axis. The clipped box hedges, which often predominate, can be so complicated that they are reminiscent of detailed embroidery (broderie). The space between the green patterns is filled in with colored earth, sand, chippings or bedding plants; rare specimens imported from distant places adorn the scene in pots and beds.

Neatly trimmed beech trees, hornbeams or lime trees lend certain parts of the garden an intimate air of privacy like that of a living-room, forming tall walls along the avenues or arching tunnels of foliage and bowers.

Trees and shrubs are trained into every possible desirable shape, subject to the architecture of the whole. "Imperfect" nature was redesigned according to the rules of art, so that it could serve man for utilitarian, instructive and entertainment purposes. After some stimulating cultural amusement, it was possible to enjoy the tranquillity of plants and flowers, water and art. The fragrances, musical notes of birdsong, the sound of fountains and the splashing of waterfalls cascading down, soothed the senses. There were small pleasures such as someone getting lost in the maze, or stepping by chance on a trick mechanism which caused a jet of water to spurt up. You could retire to a grotto of shells and imagine that you were in a fairytale world of nymphs, satyrs and imaginary creatures spouting water.

The Palace of Versailles, which belonged to Louis XIV, the powerful French Sun King, was unparalleled as a pleasure palace. True stories about grand banquets where candied fruit hung in the trees, a marzipan palace stole the show, and meat for the numerous guests was served in the rocky fissures of an artificial mountain, surpass the most decadent of fantasies. When the king was at Versailles, the gardens were transformed into a huge theater where the plays of Racine and Molière were performed and Lully's music was played. Throughout Europe, Louis' splendid garden parties were discussed in tones of awe and envy. They were a sort of psychological warfare, and under Louis XIV, France was always at war with one country or another. As a center of power, the Sun King's Palace of Versailles was unsurpassed.

This grand decor, which formed the perfect scene to bring out the qualities of Louis XIV as an absolute monarch, was designed by Le Nôtre, who worked for the king from 1661 for more than twenty years. As was often the case in those days, he had studied several branches of art before devoting himself to garden architecture. With Versailles, his name was permanently established. The gardens of this gigantic project which consumed vast amounts of money and employed legions of laborers, formed the greatest example for Europe's ruling classes during the Baroque era.

The basic ideas which Le Nôtre applied so successfully that the "French style" developed as an overwhelming movement in garden architecture, were not really new at all. The ideal of the unity of the buildings and gardens, the principles of proportion and beauty, the laws of number and size dated back to classical antiquity and had been reintroduced at the time of the Renaissance.

It was above all the sixteenth-century Italian terraced gardens, such as those of the Villa d'Este, the Villa Farnese and the Villa Lante that became famous for their architectural beauty. During the Renaissance, Italy was the leader in the field of garden architecture.

It is not surprising that important artistic movements gained an international character. Artists and craftsmen often worked at several courts and introduced the styles of their own countries. Rich young men concluded their studies with a Grand Tour of Europe, where they came into contact with Italian and French garden architecture and returned with wonderful tales about the sights they had seen. Architects and gardeners were sent away to learn from the examples of their colleagues. In addition, there were several books available in the field of garden architecture on theoretical treatises, and with designs and illustrations of decorative patterns.

Although the "French style" had permeated almost everywhere by the end of the seventeenth and the beginning of the eighteenth century, the gardens in the different European countries often retained their own character. The nature of the landscape, the mentality of the people, and the related traditions helped to determine the way in which the prevailing style was applied. The territory was by no means always large enough to extend the main axis into the surrounding countryside. In some cases smaller gardens did consist of geometrical areas, clipped box hedges and all sorts of accompanying garden ornaments, but lacked the central axis to interrelate the various elements. In this way, many variations on the architectural theme were developed.

Not everyone was charmed by such strictly designed gardens. The far-reaching formal and artificial design of the whole had been criticized for a long time before the first serious attempts were made in England in the first half of the eighteenth century to design gardens with a more "natural" and spontaneous style. Meanwhile, the bourgeoisie became more influential, liberalism flour-ished and the power of the absolute rulers slowly disintegrated. Against this background the new landscape style gradually developed. In this, England replaced France in providing the leading example in garden architecture. During the transitional phase, elements from both styles were used side by side or in combination, but at a later stage, part of the old baroque gardens had to make way for landscaped gardens.

This brought only a temporary end to the architectural approach in garden design, as became clear in the nineteenth century when garden architects once again applied the principles of the Baroque and Renaissance eras with renewed enthusiasm to create a dignified and historical setting for imposing monuments.

There are no traces left of the ebullient life which was a feature of the gardens of European courts. They no longer serve as a status symbol of the rulers, dignitaries, and wealthy citizens. The state, or the wealthy foundation which usually manages such places, has opened the gilded entrance gates to admit the public at large. Like museums and ancient monuments, these historical gardens are now part of the cultural heritage, for even if there are no coaches in the courtyard and the ladies are no longer dressed in crinolines, they still retain some of the atmosphere of the past.

In many cases restoration has succeeded in retaining the diversity which develops when a garden is influenced by different styles during the course of its long history. On the other hand, the choice of a particular period has led to the reconstruction of baroque gardens such as those at Herrenhausen in Hanover or at the Palace Het Loo in Apeldoorn. Engineers, architects, historical experts, garden designers and gardeners co-operate closely as they did in the past to recreate the gardens as the architectural whole they were intended to be long ago.

BELOEIL

Viewed from the castle, a large ornamental pool forms the beginning of a main axis which the designer extended beyond the actual gardens far into the surrounding landscape. The De Ligne family have owned the estate of Beloeil in Belgium since 1511, and it was highly regarded at several European courts. The construction of the architectural gardens in the first half of the eighteenth century further emphasized the owner's important position.

By means of an elaborate system of a main axis and transverse axes the garden conformed to the classical ideal of creating a unity between the building, the garden and the environment.

The geometrical gardens lie on either side of the large ornamental pool in which sparkling fireworks were reflected in the past during evening festivities. To the right of these there is a vegetable garden divided into rectangular sections.

BELOEIL

BELOEIL
The gardens on either side of the
pool are lined with tall hornbeam
hedges, which are so precisely clipped
that they mark out the avenues in
absolutely straight lines. Within these,
there is a series of room-like gardens.
They are surrounded by straight hedges,
carpeted with grass, adorned with ponds,
and – although every area is designed
in an individual way – always have a
purely symmetrical pattern

BAGATELLE
Amongst the close-mown lawns with apparently arbitrarily positioned shrubs, irregular flowerbeds and clumps of trees, the rosarium is the perfect example of order and symmetry. The lines are accentuated by low box hedges. Inside the beds there are roses which were awarded prizes during the inspections carried out in Bagatelle.

BAGATELLE
Part of the rose garden with a view of the orangery from the richly decorated Chinese pagoda.

The garden of the Château de Bagatelle on the edge of the Bois de Boulogne in Paris, is known as one of the first "jardins anglais" (literally, "English gardens"). This term was used in France to indicate a garden style which was no longer dominated by straight lines and symmetry, but which aimed for a more natural and spontaneous design. The jardins anglais usually contained romantic structures, such as ruins, temples, Chinese pagodas and picturesque small bridges. The design for Bagatelle dates from the second half of the eighteenth century. The architect, F.J. Bélanger, was inspired by his journeys to England, where the landscape style was developing at that time.

JARDIN THABOR

Like many gardens with a long history, the Jardin Thabor combines many developments in garden architecture. The present park, open to the public, is located is the same place as the gardens of the Abbey of St. Mélaine long ago. The monks named this highest part of the French city of Rennes after the biblical mountain of Tabor. Part of the Jardin Thabor has a geometrical design. Here the regular patterns of box hedges contrast with the pale gravel on the ground.

VERSAILLES

In order to show his guests the gardens from the most advantageous viewpoints, King Louis XIV himself wrote a visitors' guide for a tour of the gardens. The walk passed across the terraces, above the sunken orangery, from where visitors descended the steps via the right wing, and could then admire the plants in tubs placed outside the building.

The wooden tubs of the largest plants had shutters with hinges so that the earth could be replaced without any need for repotting. In addition to palm trees, pomegranates, myrtle, oleander, and many other heat-loving species which must spend the winter free of frost, the exotic collection included a large number of "orange trees." Louis XIV was

particularly fond of these because the orange fruit symbolized his power as the Sun King.

VERSAILLES
Entrance gate.

VERSAILLES
Statue of Louis XIV.   ▶

Art historians have described Versailles as "the absolute peak of baroque garden art" and "le Nôtre's greatest masterwork."

The origins of Versailles go back to Vaux-le-Vicomte, the property of the French minister of finance, Fouquet, for whom Le Nôtre designed a beautiful garden. In 1661 Fouquet inaugurated his new garden with a magnificent feast in honor of King Louis XIV. Unfortunately the king was more jealous than honored; he had Fouquet imprisoned, accused of embezzlement, and seized not only part of his possessions, but also the garden architect Le Nôtre, the painter Le Brun, and the architect Le Vau. Versailles was created under the guidance of this talented trio, as well as the architect Mansart, who was commissioned later. Versailles: the gardens of the intellect, the gardens of the mind.

Both critics and, above all, admirers, described in enormous detail the grandeur of these gardens, the countless fountains, the sweeping views contrasting with the intimate atmosphere of the enclosed "room" gardens, the splendid sculptures, the simple hunting lodge which developed in the course of the years to become a stately palace full of fine art, the perfect topiary of box hedges in the parterres, the tremendous ballets and operas with which Louis XIV – known as the Sun King – impressed his important foreign guests.

Le Nôtre, the grand master of this composition, succeeded in turning Versailles into a single grand architectural whole, in which each facet had its own place and significance. He served art and the king, and used all his insight to display the monarch's absolute power. The monarch was the focal point of the whole thing. It is no coincidence that the central axis, which links the palace and the gardens, runs in an east-west direction. There is a good reason why the entrance gate to the front courtyard is gilded and decorated with a sun shield. When the sun rises, it first casts a golden glow over the gate, and then moves from east to west, reaching the Sun King's bedchamber just at the right time to illuminate his daily morning rituals.

V ERSAILLES
Group of statues in silhouette.

V ERSAILLES
The decorative box parterres were copied throughout Europe, following the creation of Versailles, and were characteristic of the French style. Nowadays the areas between the patterns of clipped box hedges are filled with modern bedding plants.

In the seventeenth century the plants did not bloom so profusely and had fewer vibrant colors. Le Nôtre did not favor a surfeit of color, and although the king disagreed with his garden architect on this point, the large box parterres close to the palace were designed in subtle nuances of color.

VERSAILLES ▶

Borders with high orangery plants, showing the orangery, the low building partly concealed behind the tubs of plants, and the palace in the background.

Versailles once had a dizzying number of fountains. Because there was a lack of water – particularly in the early years – they were turned on only at certain times of the year. When Louis XIV followed his planned route, attendants passed whistled signals to let each other know that the king was on his way, so that each fountain he passed could be switched on in good time. Even now the use of water is restricted. When the fountain in the Bassin d'Apollo illustrated here is turned on, the gushing water seems to bring to life Apollo and his fiery horses. The pool from which Apollo rises up as the driver of the sun chariot – another reference to the Sun King's power – was designed by Le Brun, "the art dictator," who was the chief supervisor of all the statues in the gardens.

VERSAILLES

Box parterres and expanses of water are essential elements in Le Nôtre's overall plan. A lot of money was spent in particular on the larger expanses of water. An entire regiment of Swiss Guards was brought in to dig the Pièce de l'Eau des Suisses, which was created in 1678. The longest arm is more than a mile long from the Grand Canal, where the Sun King had spectacles performed and organized gondola trips by moonlight.

A great deal of capital and man hours were also invested in the leafy woods around the gardens. Like the buildings, the parterres, the expanses of water and the statues, they also formed part of the detailed overall plan, and comprise mature trees, many of which died off when they were transported from distant regions and were then replaced.

VERSAILLES ▶
Statue of Cyparissus and his deer.

VILLANDRY

Château Villandry is one of the great sights in the valley of the Loire in France. The castle dates from 1536 and was built in the renaissance style. In the sixteenth century its gardens were famous far and wide, and the vegetable garden in particular attracted great praise for combining practical and aesthetic factors.

When the Spaniard Joachim Carvallo occupied the property in 1906, little remained of the original design. The restoration work which endeavored to re-establish the original values continued until 1918. A book by the French architect, Du Cerceau, dating from the sixteenth century, was very valuable to Carvallo as a source of information. The engravings in this book gave a good impression of the layout, patterns and ornaments in historic French renaissance gardens such as Villandry and Blois.

The fact that careful historical studies were made did not prevent the owner's own artistic ideas from playing a role in the new design of the gardens. For example, according to art historians, the extensive clipped box hedges would not have been found in the original renaissance gardens.

VILLANDRY

The garden is designed on three levels. From the highest point there is a panoramic view of the ornamental gardens on the second level and the beautiful vegetable garden on the lowest level.

C ICHORIUM INTYBUS "RADICCIO"
Red chicory or radiccio rosso, a type
of lettuce, is eminently suitable for
introducing variations of color into a
vegetable garden.

B RASSICA
The same applies to ornamental
cabbages, of which there are several
varieties.

▶

◀

V ILLANDRY
A visit to the potager or vegetable
garden at Villandry reveals that the
cultivation of vegetables certainly does
not have to be boring. It is divided into
nine square compartments in which the
beds are arranged according to different
patterns, taking into account not only
practical considerations, but also form
and color, creating an imaginative layout
of plants which contrasts attractively with
the straight lines of the design.

BAYREUTH, EREMITAGE
Before the Countess
Wilhelmina moved into the
Neues Schloss it served as an
aviary and orangery.
Wilhelmina, the wife of Count
Georg Wilhelm von
Brandenberg-Bayreuth, used
her innate artistic talents to
enhance the gardens of the
Eremitage with grottoes, a
Roman ruin where open air
performances were held, and a
large expanse of water with
beautiful statues and fountains,
amongst other things.

BAYREUTH, EREMITAGE

▼

BAYREUTH, EREMITAGE
The semi-circular Neues Schloss is striking because of its wealth of decoration and attention to detail, which is characteristic of the German high baroque and rococo style.
In contrast, the Altes Schloss on the same estate, is reminiscent of a monastery. Count Georg Wilhelm von Brandenberg-Bayreuth had it built in 1715, long before he married Wilhelmina in 1731. He used the Eremitage as a retreat and as a place for contemplation, and even seems to have walked round, dressed in a monk's habit, with his court. Withdrawing from the decadent world with all its plots and intrigues, was a favorite pastime of many rulers. This is why it was called the Eremitage or Hermitage (literally the abode of a hermit), a term often found in the history of garden architecture.

PAPAVER
SOMNIFERUM
"PAEONIFLOWERED"

HERRENHAUSEN

The history of Herrenhausen as a comprehensive complex of gardens only really started when Duchess Sophie, the granddaughter of the English king, James I, chose the estate as her summer residence in 1680. Shortly afterwards, the Frenchman Martin Charbonnier designed the garden in the French style. For Sophie the creation was not yet complete. As was usual at that time, this was followed by constant periods of expansion and improvement. The Duchess had spent the years of her youth at the court of the family of Orange, and she saw to it that her gardeners were inspired by Dutch garden architecture. After her death there were no great changes in the gardens. This meant that they could be restored in the 1930s without too many great changes, but bombing in the Second World War caused enormous damage. Because of the large-scale restoration – which restored the original magnificence of the Grossen Garten in Herrenhausen – Hanover in Germany now prides itself on having one of the most authentic baroque gardens.

TULIPA "WEBER'S PARROT"

Tulips were first cultivated in Europe in the mid-sixteenth century. These bulbs from Persia and Turkey became so enormously popular that the trade in tulips assumed mad proportions and a single bulb sometimes sold for two to four thousand guilders. Speculation was prohibited (1635-1637), but the interest continued. More and more "wild" species were cultivated, and the number of unusual varieties steadily grew. In the second half of the seventeenth century, bicolored flamed tulips ("broken" tulips) and particularly "parrot tulips," with their unusually shaped petals, were particularly popular.

HERRENHAUSEN

H ERRENHAUSEN
At one time, every self-respecting garden owner with sufficient means had an open air theater designed for his garden. The theater in Herrenhausen is surrounded by hedges and was created in 1689-1693. It is one of the oldest. Nowadays performances are put on there once again. The effect of depth of the performing area, which is more than 164 feet long, is further reinforced by two lines of gilded statues and yew pyramids. Clipped beeches form the wings on either side of the garden theater. The deep amphitheater where the audience is seated lies beyond the area illustrated in this photograph. ▼

HERRENHAUSEN

The "parterre à oranges" lies in front of the Gallery where Duchess Sophie exhibited her art treasures. As in medieval monastic gardens, the orange trees in terracotta pots were arranged on squares, like a chess board.

HERRENHAUSEN

One of the transverse axes consists of successive pools in which jets of water gush up from forty fountains. The Great Fountain lies on the main axis in another part of the garden, designed to attract respect when it was designed. Water from the River Leine was transported to reservoirs via an aqueduct. However, despite advice from French, Dutch and Italian water engineers, it was initially impossible to force the water up to a great height. It was only in 1720 that the jet of water from the fountain rose higher than one hundred feet, which was greatly admired by visitors. Nowadays the Great Fountain of Herrenhausen is the tallest garden fountain in Europe, reaching a height of 260 feet.

H ERMANSTAL (KASSEL) ▲
Golden reflections, blue sky, and
stone statues evoke an image of a long-
past and turbulent era.

H ERMANSTAL

SANS SOUCI

The six tiered terraces of Sans Souci (Potsdam), which is about 19 miles outside Berlin, have been beautifully restored. On either side of the monumental staircase they form a balanced pattern of niches and climbing plants. After every level covered in climbing plants, there is a niche with heat-loving plants, protected by a glass window. Frederick II of Prussia had the terraces constructed in 1744 in order to protect sensitive peach trees and vines against the cold.

S ANS SOUCI
Chinese tea house.

S ANS SOUCI
In the course of the eighteenth century, new areas were constantly added to the original design for Sans Souci, designed in different styles. The Chinese Tea House is also eighteenth century. "Chinoiserie" – the fashionable way in which gardens were embellished with Chinese-style structures - had reached a peak.

SCHLOSS BELVEDERE
Agaves in pots set up outside the orangery.

SCHLOSS BELVEDERE
Work on the gardens of Schloss Belvedere in Weimar started in 1724. As is the case with the neighboring Schloss Tiefurt, Countess Anna Amalia also made her mark on this large estate for a long time. At a later stage the gardens were modified in accordance with the English landscape style. The modern (restored) gardens have re-established part of the original baroque design.

SCHLOSS TIEFURT
In the eighteenth and nineteenth centuries an important part of German cultural and religious life took place in the city of Weimar. Life at the court flourished and monumental buildings rose up in and around the city. The gardens of Schloss Tiefurt developed in the curve of the River Ilm under the influence of this positive climate. Christoph Wieland, founder of the Sturm-und-Drang movement – and the poet/philosopher Goethe, visited the castle at the time when Countess Anna Amalia ruled.
After the gardens fell into neglect, the landscape architect, Eduard Petzold, worked on their re-establishment from 1845-1850. Tiefurt was extensively restored in about 1970.

HAMPTON COURT, PALACE GARDENS
Ornamental gardens with patterns of pruned herbs as well as box trees.

HAMPTON COURT, PALACE GARDENS

It is not surprising that the important centers of power in Europe changed with the coming and going of rulers and historical movements. For example, Hampton Court and the Palace Gardens on the Thames were a reflection of the time. When the powerful Henry VIII (1492-1547) had the gardens designed, he wished to have a view of the ornamental gardens from his windows, like his French rival, King Francois I, and this is what happened. The frivolous King Charles II (1630-1685) added, amongst other things, the Grand Canal, and the "patte d'oie," the three radiating avenues of lime trees to the east of the palace. However, when Mary Stuart and the Dutch stadtholder William III succeeded to the throne in 1689, the gardens enjoyed their heyday. Hampton Court wished to compare with the great baroque examples in France, both in its new construction by Sir Christopher Wren, and in the design of the gardens.

Hampton Court contained everything which belonged in palace gardens of great standing: complicated, intricate parterres by Daniel Marot, a name which is also found in the history of Het Loo, yew trees pruned into pyramid shapes, baroque statuary, a wilderness of copses, a maze and glittering fountains.

Shortly after the death of William III, Queen Anne changed as much of the palace gardens as she could. It is said that she hated her brother-in-law so much that she did not wish to be reminded of him in any way.

CASTLE HOWARD

View of the magnificent late baroque castle by the architect-garden designer, Sir John Vanbrugh (1664-1726). The gigantic Atlas fountain in the foreground has embellished the buildings of Castle Howard in the county of Yorkshire (England) only since the end of the nineteenth century.

RANUNCULUS ASIATICUS HYBRIDS

PAPAVER SOMNIFERUM "PAEONIFLOWERED" HYBRID

Since the end of the Middle Ages there has been a steady growth of interest in decorative plants, eventually leading to an international collecting mania. In the seventeenth century, both experts and wealthy amateurs traveled long distances to acquire rare specimens which were enthusiastically cultivated and cross-fertilized to produce new varieties and colors. Double flowers with smooth, round or fringed petals in pastel shades were particularly popular, such as peonies, roses, buttercups, and peony-like poppies, which are often depicted in seventeenth-century still lifes of flowers .

RANUNCULUS ASIATICUS HYBRIDS

The buttercup originates from Asia Minor. In about 1580 the plant was introduced in western Europe from Turkey by Carolus Clusius, who was in contact with botanists throughout Europe and introduced a large number of new plants.

ROSA CENTIFOLIA "CRISTATA"

The fragrant centifolia roses are also known as the "Dutch Rose" and the "Rose des Peintres" (the painters' rose). They are depicted on paintings of flowers by seventeenth-century Dutch masters. It is probable that this type of rose was produced by cross pollination at the end of the sixteenth century.

BANTRY HOUSE

Bantry House is in southwest Ireland on Bantry Bay, and because of the mild climate, all sorts of heat-loving plants are able to grow there. In the mid-nineteenth century, terraces with balustrades were built in the part of the garden overlooking the bay. The enclosed part behind the house had the characteristics of a French renaissance garden. In order to bring out the specific character of old houses and castles, nineteenth-century garden architects often turned to examples from the Renaissance and Baroque eras, and Italian and French styles were revived. They borrowed the basic ideas from old books of examples, but because of their own interpretation and use of plants the gardens had a contemporary character at the same time as a historical one.

GIARDINO GIUSTI

Giardino Giusti is situated on a steep slope on the east of the River Adige, and there is a splendid view of the surrounding area from the highest point. Large terracotta pots, statues and elegant stone fountains were placed at the intersections of the paths. When the renaissance garden was replaced by a new design in the nineteenth century, little remained of the original layout other than the lyrical descriptions of John Evelyn, Thomas Coryat, Goethe and other celebrated visitors. During the restoration an attempt was made to restore as much as possible of the original sixteenth-century design. Only a few of the ancient cypresses have survived, but the specimens planted later will also border the avenues with their slender pillars.

GIARDINO GIUSTI

GIARDINO GIUSTI

The character of a garden is determined not only by the fashion of the time, but certainly also by the atmosphere of a particular region, the climate and the vegetation. In Giardino Giusti – a famous Italian renaissance garden in Verona – the charm and elegance of the cypresses always attracted the praise of visitors. For centuries, Giardino Giusti was famous for its beauty, both in Italy and abroad. The garden of the villa was commissioned by the influential Agostino Giusti in the second half of the sixteenth century; the original design of the terraces, the layout and the patterns used were characteristic of the time.

GIARDINO GIUSTI

VILLA BETTONI (BOLIAGO, LAGO DI GARDA)

R<small>OSA HYBRID</small>

ROSA CENTIFOLIA "PARVIFLORA"

Roses have been cultivated and admired since ancient times, but planting them in beds and borders on a large scale did not take place until the nineteenth and twentieth centuries. The rose had already been used as a flowering shrub or hedge and had been planted as a climber on walls and trellises, or trained along poles, as in the gardens of Het Loo. The roses had to be fragrant as well as beautiful, because the scent of the flowers, as well as delightful sounds, formed an important aspect of the pleasures of the garden.

L UNARIA ANNUA "ALBA"
The white flowers of "honesty" in a flowerbed
surrounded by a box hedge forms a serene and balanced
design which enhances the appearance of the garden as a
whole.

BEECKESTEYN

BEECKESTEYN

The design of Beeckesteyn (Velzen) has been influenced by various different styles of garden architecture over the course of the years. In the second half of the seventeenth century strictly geometrical structures were introduced. When the property had fallen into decay and passed to the municipality of Velzen it was restored, and the house became a museum in 1969.

The sculptures which were added after the restoration include a statue of Venus, abducted by Vulcan. In the background, part of the old wall can be seen where the branches of fruit trees were trained in the past.

BEECKESTEYN

There is a large ornamental pool at the intersection of the main axes and transverse axes. A survey of the design dating from the 1780s indicates that the pool was a dominant element in the gardens of Beeckesteyn. During this period the owner, Jacob Boreel, had the park redesigned by the architect, Johann Georg Michael, who built the further reaches of the gardens in accordance with the landscape style which was fashionable at the time.

HET LOO
An aerial view clearly shows how the sections of a geometric garden are combined into a whole by means of a system of axes. The central axis of Het Loo runs from north to south. At the northern end three avenues radiate from a central point to the surrounding area, a pattern known as "patte d'oie" (literally: goose foot). The line from the central avenue continues through the front courtyard and the palace into the central axis, which successively dissects the lower and upper gardens and has an optical end in the semicircular gallery of pillars (colonnade).

On either side of the palace lie the King's and Queen's Gardens.

HET LOO
The Lower Garden is composed of eight parterres, two "topiary" parterres dominated by box topiary, and two grass parterres on either side of the main axis. In order to give a vertical accent to the level areas, the outer margins (plate-bandes) are planted with yew trees clipped in pyramid shapes. In the Queen's Gardens there are rows of plants in tubs, also pruned into distinctive shapes.

The area between the artistic box figures is filled with different colored gravel and brick. It is worth noting that the plants in the plate-bandes are not arranged close together as they often were in French gardens, but were spaced far apart in the old Dutch style, so that the special shape of each plant could come into its own.

HET LOO

The edges of the parterres along the straight main axis are decorated with narrow canals. The Venus fountain is in the background.

In 1684 Stadtholder William III bought a small castle in the neighborhood of Apeldoorn, surrounded by forests and dunes, an excellent hunting area which enabled him to withdraw from his exhausting political and military life from time to time. During the years that followed, the new palace was built and a start was made on the geometric gardens. When William III married Mary Stuart in 1689 and became

King of England, both the palace and the gardens had to be adapted to his new status. On this occasion the so-called Upper Garden was added to Het Loo, amongst other things. The architect, Jacob Roman, supervised the construction of the palace, and he was probably also responsible for the overall design of the gardens. Although Het Loo is considerably smaller than, for example, the gardens of Versailles, and contains typically Dutch stylistic characteristics, the influence of the baroque garden style is clearly present. There were plenty of signs of the expertise and knowledge of the great French examples in the courts of the House of Orange. One of William's most important confidants had studied the style extensively on his travels, and in addition there was the contribution from artists such as the French Huguenot, Daniel Marot. When the Huguenots were outlawed in France, this engraver and decorator, like many of his fellow believers, fled to safer regions and was employed by the stadtholder, who attached great

importance to the freedom of religious expression. Marot designed the elegant box topiary of the parterres. The garden was completed in 1692.

Over the centuries, new developments in garden architecture completely replaced the seventeenth-century beginnings, until a large-scale renovation, which lasted from 1979-1984, restored the old gardens to their former splendor.

A close study of the source material and archaeological finds made it possible not only to reconstruct the overall design with the appropriate ornaments, but also to get close to the colors and shapes of the original seventeenth-century plants.

Only occasionally were concessions made to the more recent past, for example, in the Upper Garden, some valuable trees from the landscape period were spared.

The pool with the Venus fountain is situated at the point where the central axis passes through the Lower Garden. It contains Venus with Cupid on a pedestal decorated with shells and coral, surrounded by gilded tritons, reeds and swans. The heralds of the sea – the tritons – are blowing their horns. They have human torsos and the lower body of a fish.

The original statue of Venus, who was the mother of nature and protectress of gardens as well as the goddess of love, was made by the late baroque sculptor from Brussels, Gabriël Grupello.

HET LOO
Detail of the Venus fountain.

HET LOO

The Queen's Garden included an intimate area known as the "Queen's Cabinet," consisting of an inner and outer berceau. The berceau or leafy avenue was often used in architecturally designed gardens to visually close off part of the garden, and usually included bowers with passages and seats. During the restoration of Het Loo the framework along which the foliage was trained was made of hardwood. According to a seventeenth-century description, the leafy avenues were planted with elm at that time, but in order to avoid the risk of Dutch Elm disease it was decided to use a hornbeam hedge this time (Carpinus betulus).

HET LOO

Two beautiful waterfalls have been constructed on the bank on either side of the garden. At the bottom of the Cascade of Narcissus the well-known mythological figure is reflected on the surface of the water, while the water behind him streams down in steps from pool to pool. Cascades or waterfalls were important elements in the static architectural gardens of the Baroque and Renaissance eras. They were incorporated in Italian renaissance gardens, such as those of the Villa Torlonia, the Villa Lante and the Palazzo Farnese. The most spectacular example must be the cascade at Wilhelmsehohe in Germany, where the water falls more than six hundred feet.

HET LOO

Each of the four grass parterres in the Lower Garden is adorned with a sculpture from Greek mythology: Apollo with a lyre (see illustration), Pomona, Bacchus and Flora. These garden statues serve not only to reinforce the geometry, but also to say something about the owner of the garden and the lessons of nature. For example, the four above-mentioned statues can be related to the virtues of William III as a peace-loving ruler. The clipped box hedges of the grass parterres are surrounded by bands of sand which facilitate maintenance. At various points there are painted poles for training roses and other climbing and trained plants.

HET LOO

The area surrounding the palace was not only densely forested, but also contained many sources of water. The water was transported to Het Loo from various different locations via a network of wooden, stone and lead pipes to feed all the fountains, cascades and jets of water. Before renovating the system of pipes, the restorers calculated as accurately as possible the water capacity necessary for each element, and formed a plan of the original waterworks on the basis of authentic descriptions, drawings and excavations, so that this could be reconstructed as accurately as possible. For example, the amount of water needed for the Hercules fountain (bottom right) was estimated at about four gallons of water per hour.

WELDAM CASTLE

At the end of the nineteenth century, when many of the old geometric gardens of Europe had been replaced by the landscape style, there was an upsurge of interest in the garden architecture of the past. Architectural gardens based on the seventeenth-century example were planted alongside many historical buildings. In many cases they also had the personal stamp of the nineteenth-century architect.

The estate of Weldam Castle in Overijssel, which was still surrounded by avenues of trees and a rectangular system of canals, in accordance with Dutch tradition, was given a baroque character at that time. The layout, dating from 1886, was designed by the French architect, Edouard André, and was executed by his apprentice and colleague, H.A.C. Poortman.

WELDAM CASTLE

The elegant topiary parterres, which were planted at the front of the castle in the early twentieth century, have now been replaced by subsequent alterations. However, what remains of this period – such as the impressive topiary and the 460-foot-long leafy avenue – was well worth retaining.

TWICKEL
This berry-bearing yew tree is one of the many living ornaments in the garden in Twickel (Overijssel). They include the most bizarre works of art in the field of topiary, which are all pruned with equal precision. Twickel and Weldam Castle (see p. 54) are often mentioned together because the team of Poortman and André brought the style of days long gone back to life in a very individual way.

ZUYLESTEIN CASTLE (Leersum)
Flowering perennials, as well as tall annuals and the occasional thistle, rise up above the robust clipped box hedges. Behind this lies the medieval castle which had to be reconstructed from its foundations after being destroyed by bombs in the Second World War.

WILHERING ABBEY

Border plants, including red salvias, grey-leaved betony, yellow marigolds, and roses.

SCHÖNBRUNN

From the ornamental pool an avenue with trimmed walls of trees affords a view of the palace designed by the famous Austrian baroque architect, J.B. Fischer van Erlach. For centuries the imperial pleasure palace of Schönbrunn in Vienna was owned by the Habsburgs, once one of Europe's greatest and most influential families.

The euphoria of victory, following the liberation of Vienna after the seige by the Turks, led to an enormous growth of monumental buildings and gardens in and around the city towards the end of the seventeenth century. Fischer von Erlach was commissioned to design Schönbrunn in such a way that it would bear comparison with the palace of Versailles of his rival, Louis XIV. Before becoming the court architect of the Habsburg rulers, Leopold I, Joseph I and Charles VI, he had already built up a career in Italy, where he had been apprenticed to the great master, Bernini. At that time the whole complex – consisting of the palace, garden and park – had a larger surface area than the city of Vienna. Work on the gardens started at the beginning of the eighteenth century, and the appearance of the park and gardens was influenced over the years by various Habsburg rulers, garden architects and period styles.

SCHÖNBRUNN

Elaborate scaffolding is required to clip the famous hedges of Schönbrunn. The work is made even more difficult by the fact that the hedges contain many niches where statues are displayed. The maintenance not only of Schönbrunn, but of all reconstructed or original formal gardens, is extremely labor intensive. The geometric layout means that the garden should always look extremely well groomed. For example, the borders must be edged with the greatest precision, because any deviation would disrupt the original pattern of parterres and flowerbeds. In many cases the geometry of the garden requires that all the small trees, trimmed in pyramid or spherical shapes, should be exactly the same size. Clipping the box hedges also particularly demands a great deal of attention and expertise.

SCHÖNBRUNN
A view through two trellised gates of treillage, the French term for trellises. In geometric gardens there were often separate areas of trellises, frequently connected with other elements for dividing up or enclosing areas, such as hedges, leafy avenues and pergolas. The often richly adorned trellis originally consisted of painted wood, but in the late seventeenth and early eighteenth centuries it was also frequently made of iron.

SCHÖNBRUNN

SCHÖNBRUNN

One part of the gardens is dominated by close-mown lawns with artistically designed garlands of flowers and circular flowerbeds.

(The large-scale intricate parterres on either side of the main axis behind the palace, which is 512 feet wide, provide another view. Here the original French influence can still be identified, even though the plants are clearly from a later date. The basic plan of the gardens was drawn up by Fischer von Erlach, and the details were elaborated by French architects. From 1744, Maria Theresa had many changes made, although the original French style was retained. Her husband, Franz I, had a particular interest in exotic plants. He entrusted his collection to two Dutch gardeners, one of whom traveled to the Caribbean to import new plants for the large orangery (dating from 1744). In later times, Schonbrunn also kept up with current developments, and in the twentieth century it expanded to become one of Vienna's main public attractions.

S CHÖNBRUNN

S CHÖNBRUNN

BUSSACO

BUSSACO

An elegant parterre garden lies in front of the romantic palace of Bussaco in Portugal, now a hotel. The compartments are filled with silvery-grey betony (Stachys lanata), which harmonizes with the dark green of the elegant pattern of low box hedges.

BUSSACO

BUSSACO

NATIONAL PARK OF QUELUZ

Together with the palace, the gardens of Queluz, to the west of the Portuguese capital of Lisbon, form a perfect example of elegance and graceful dignity. They were designed by the Frenchman, Jean-Baptiste Robillon, and commissioned by Dom Pedro III and his wife, Maria I. The period of construction encompassed almost thirty years from 1753 to 1782. Many of the elements composing the garden – the rococo style fountains, the special parterre construction, the areas of water, colorful tiles and glazed earthenware made in Portugal, and statues of Italian origin – are admirable works of art in themselves.

NATIONAL PARK OF QUELUZ

The parterre of continuous foliage is divided into compartments by small straight paths. They radiate outwards towards a group of statues – an architectural device to focus the attention on a work of art.

The narrow, vertical cypresses give an extra dimension to the geometrical garden; they have a natural pillar shape, which is used in garden architecture to introduce vertical accents.

NATIONAL PARK OF QUELUZ

NATIONAL PARK OF QUELUZ

The steps of the staircase, bridging the difference in level between the building and the garden, have a powerful spatial effect. The lines are accentuated by a strong contrast between light and dark, caused by the bright sunlight entering the garden.

In Portugal there are many places where geometric figures are set in lines; cubes, trapezia and balls of box, yew, privet or heat-loving camellia. This topiary forms part of the Portuguese tradition and is not always related to the strict mathematical principles of the Baroque era, in which every little tree and every hedge had a shape imposed on it, based on set sizes and proportions.

HOTEL SINTRA / PÁLACIO DE SETEAIS

Art lovers from all over the world settled for many years in the mountainous region surrounding the Portuguese town of Sintra, so that they could create their own earthly paradise in the midst of the picturesque landscape. The Pálacio de Seteais is a palace comprising two buildings built in approximately 1800 and nowadays used as a hotel. From here there is a view over part of the garden, the geometric character of which is determined by the typical Portuguese topiary. The Atlantic Ocean lies in the hazy distance, far beyond the valley and woods.

PRIVATE GARDEN, SINTRA

HOTEL BOM JESUS DO MONTE

High above the tower blocks of the city of Braga in Portugal, the gardens of Bom Jesus form an oasis of peace. On certain days of the year, particularly at Whitsun, there is a very different atmosphere in the area around Braga. Thousands of pilgrims travel to Bom Jesus do Monte, where seemingly infinite steep steps lead up to the church on the top of the "holy mountain." These famous steps – a glorious monument of baroque architecture – were built between approximately 1735 and 1774.

B_{OM JESUS}